AVENUE
DREAD

Order this book online at www.trafford.com
or email orders@trafford.com

Most Trafford titles are also available at major online book retailers.

Print information available on the last page.

ISBN: 978-1-4251-1997-3 (sc)
ISBN: 978-1-4269-3965-5 (e)

Trafford rev. 08/11/2023

Trafford
PUBLISHING®   www.trafford.com
North America & international
toll-free: 844-688-6899 (USA & Canada)
fax: 812 355 4082

AVENUE
DREAD

Michael Angel

Table of Contents

AVENUE DREAD

Down on the avenue
There lived a little boy
He picked all his victims
Then proceeded to say

Once upon a time
In a dark and lonely place
Despair had overcome
His dark sullen face

A moment of awareness
A taste of sour dread
A kitchen in a house
On an inner suburban spread

———

WORD SONG

Never so much emphasis on a word
Soft spoken bird
Discovery is yours
Dark shadows cover
A journey through perception

The house on the hill
Stood old and glowing
With moonlight that hung in the sky
The little girl's shapely menace
Stood hauntingly in the doorway
Her look enticed
Some aspire to surprise

Have you ever had the feeling
Of strangeness dawn upon you
Like the subtle perfume of raw lust

———

DISDAIN

What a bounty
This thing called destiny
It leads me down a path
Not travelled, unknown
Feel your heart pulling away

Disdain

Everything here is so real
I cannot think only feel
Feel each breath
Each new test

———

BLOODY OYSTER

The ridiculously absurd
Preposterous play continued
It was his life
Unfolding like a tragic play
For everyone to see
Think of where you want to be
In your dreams at night you will see
That life is a bloody oyster

———

MURKY GREEN ROSE

Look into the sea
Of murky discontent
See all that you would feel
In a single rose
As it transposed
My mind did close
Into yours

Nobody likes to fight
Unless they can win
That's why they need so much more
You feel it
When you feel the sting

Open awareness
Feelings that drift
Lukewarm friends
Arrive in spring
The new moon dawns
Awaken to heat
Feel your breath
Feel your feet

———

GOING DOWN

Pick up the feeling
From thin air
Start to breathe
Repeatedly stare

A reaching future
That exists in the past
Is showing its teeth
At last

Where does reality hide
In what frame of mind
Do you reside
Swampy creepy marsh
Fog rises from the grass
Time is a feeling
A feeling that lasts

A prolonged state of awareness
Manipulative and ever-changing
It just keeps on raining
The Goddess of love
Is she here to hurt me
I'm going down
To see what's there

———

OTHER SIDE

I live in the back streets
At night I sleep
With periscopic eyes
I shoot sheep

The secret self
That hides within us all
A moment of reality
Feel its presence fall

What would it take
To bring on this state
For a lasting time

———

CROSSFIRE

We are a hedonistic society
We're here we're real
We refuse to yield

It's been years since I have been this close
To the feeling I thought I had lost
Old memories linger on
A heavy sigh is all that lies
Between you and it
A second split into two
An emotional hue
A wondrous state
Of love and hate

Separation of the self
Stringent boundaries of emotional control
Demons roam free within every soul

———

FEELINGS

When I'm close to you
I feel like something's new
Something real
But not yet sealed

Feelings unspoken
They exist in the air
But nobody notices
Them there

———

LOVE'S JEWEL

The silhouette of her earthly embrace
Hung desperately in the light
Of an orange full moon

Dare I pass into the darkness
Brilliant majestic light
Shine on me tonight
Lead me into the dark
For my love
For the ark

A stunning jewel
Hanging there taunting me
So you do feel something
In your secret private world

Cool crazy cat
Wish you were that
A complex stream
Of endeavour and dreams

———

DEMONS

Brief glimpses of understanding
Surface
Out of the cold hard rage
Of demons
That dwells in my soul

This desperate urge to understand
This glue of love
If it comes undone
The demons reign

With the monsters at the helm
Life becomes a private hell
Gone is the sweet fragrant love
That bought happiness and meaning
I cannot believe it came apart so easily

———

WAR WITH LOVE

She's my baby, she'll be forever, but now she's gone
She'll pick you up, weave you in and drag your heart
along
She came inside with velvet gloves
Still so ripe so untouched
How can you believe in love so much

In the war with love
I fell in love
The front has broken
Silent words are spoken

Ever since the world began
Man has learnt to be a man
Travelled through his night filled days
Always seems to find the way
In this land this promised land
She reaches out with her hand
And if she leaves I never will believe
That she is gone
For if she's free we live in peace, you see
She can't be wrong

I want to be free
I want you to be
Come, dance, here with me
Celebrate love and if you should need
I'll be ready to bleed
Mi amor es mi curazon.

HUNGRY HOUNDS

Can you see the pain of loneliness in their eyes
The accelerated pounding
Of a blissfully contented heart
Startles subtle senses
Fine acute
The slightest sound
Can be so smooth
Exotic delights are tripled with speed
Silent applause rings true
So do the hungry hounds
That lap at the tides
Of murky discontent

———

ROSE

We love to love fragrant roses
Our thoughts transpose us
Delicate beauties tantalize and entice us
In this comfort zone of climate control
I try not to hold onto too much
It's such a rush

We're just playing, push too far
I'm not saying, nearest star
Far off limits undesigned
Crave for fields of pure sunshine
What crazy wings would we have to wear
To get to a place as far away
As nowhere
What do I have to say
To convey
The emotions that I feel
This has to be real
The begging of the rest of your life
Is only a heartbeat away
Sequenced words of glitter and dust
Come on child let's self combust
Fickle child born too wild
Runs hot and cold
Far to young way too old

———

LEECH

A lone man watches paradise
Through his bug stained windscreen
A thought rushes in, it begins
Feeling good is never enough
Subtle greed, a sensuous touch
How do you find inspiration
Can you make it pay
The empty hour, the endless moment
The power of thought
Succumb to time's subtle embrace
To sit in one place
Causes you to feel
The perception of being
Life's good enough but a dream is nicer
Thoughts and feelings in your mind
Memories collide into time
The endless moment lingers on
A decade's vibe in your bones

———

WAGE SLAVE

Casual love just slide right by
Don't stop to long this world has died
True love was once known
When wild wolves roamed
In the untamed passion of the night

Nothing is like that today
We live in a prison
No reason for us to shine
The lights of the city
Do it just fine

We are a consequence of a structure
Forming itself around us
Not regarding us
It cares for it's wealthy
Not the children in the street

A demon of concrete and steel
Only willing to deal
With the currency it made
So we would always have to slave

———

FANTASTIC REALITY

Dirty ashes on my page
Re-light the joint in a haze
Open up to total truth
Why hide facts that seem uncouth

Wipe the ashes from the page
Head the words of all the mighty mage
Fantasy, it has to be
Reality, is into me
Complexity

The complex wonderment
Of an intricate reality
It has to be
Good for me
Anarchy

———

17

SHOW AND TELL

What words could escape me now
In this golden moment
This golden life

A gentle sigh passes through his eyes
What of this gentle sigh
This abstract feeling

The spirit of the future has dawned on us
It's opened the door to set up a score
Is what to come already been
Does she love me
Or is it a dream

All material things sought
In the end equal naught
Seek that which you would keep
That you would take
That special prize
At death's golden gate

———

QUEST

Delusions of madness
Find true meaning
What forces could shape thought
Is what to be
Already perceived
What of deceit
Trickery could arise

I see through you
My dearest self
I understand your pain
And feel your happiness
I often wonder if you know me

Icy and dark
This pain is by far the worst
How much must I endure
Until I can hold my love
Year after year

———

PARAMOUR

Lives colliding, friction fighting
A jealous tension where love sleeps
Trying to awaken from suspended animation

A series of striking blows
It begins to show
Because caring is too hard
The political structure is sometimes so complex
We forget what's best

Now its hard, now its core
Come on baby, let's score
Caution sees what bravado does not
What does it mean
Each word
Each scene

Nothing could be so intense
Nothing less would she accept
Stone petalled diamond
The shinning won't relent
Each moment, each breath

REALITY CHECK

It's as if life were a play
We its players
Strictly abiding to a set script
With genuine fear there to abhor you

Nobody can deny what really is
That is you as seen through His eyes
There is no disguise that can hide
What is really true about you inside

With the barriers all lifted
We feel what really is
The pill, a delicious treat
Acceptance is yours
My sweet

———

THE CELESTIAL INTELLIGENCE

The soul is inspired by music
Long empirical silences
Perfectly ordered world of escape
The bedroom for the bedroom's sake

Directions to the road of success
Please don't tell the rest
They will rush there

The animal beast lives between us
Esperanto
Try for the endless high
For the lover's art
For the delicate touch
Of a dove's heart

It so easy to go astray
Each moment new thoughts lead the way
Continental cologne where beauty lies
Even where you dare to look

Why should we consent
To just any old puppet
We can't understand it
Each new pact
Must be exact

Time to change, rearrange
All that is known
Into the wind
The night is full blown
Bring me this creature of the night
Without the sting without respite
Indelicate beings of water and ice
Proper and prim lets be concise
Prepare the device
My order at last

Each perceptual recognition
Sparks designers
Masters of a race
Did they leave no trace

————

CIRCLE

Enjoy the sacred stick
Smoke it with exalted bliss
Easy in the arms
Of this calculated risk

You have become your sacred host
A master of yourself
The centre of focus
Is a solid packed bong
Whirling in a circle of love

Time evolves you
Then involves you
Every one of you

For what is a part
Without its sum
The dream we dreamt
Has come undone

Melting moments
Of delicate taste
Don't wait to long
Break, make haste

―――――

ORANGE MOON

I saw you walk past
From the corner of my eye
Your incredible golden love
Held in my heart

In an instant I knew it was you
I was not aware of the moment
When I realized she was there
I could hardly breathe

Her beautiful flowing hair
The scent of her wildly passionate body
Sent my heart to heaven

While looking for inspiration
I try not to fall
Long hot summer days have arrived
A certain number in a year
She's around but not really here

The madness was but a gift
The anger just a rift
I think of her everyday
And with each passing thought
My love grows for her in so many ways

She left with the orange full moon
The rift would approach all too soon

———

THIN ICE

A multitude of icy paths stretched out
In every possible direction
All searching for a destination
Some new and inspired
Others old and tired

What do they hope to find
At the end of that icy line
We have abstract fields
Green pills
Love is put to the test
Tread lightly I stress
The ice is thin
At best

———

MOMENTS

You melt in my arms
Like an exotic delight
Soft as the morning light

I can look out my window
I can see
The misty morning air
Your reflection melts into me

To receive a kiss
As blessed as this
Is beyond compare
Don't you ask
Don't you dare

———

GHOST

A darkened room in a large old house
Is filled with the light
Of an orange full moon

Dwelling in the attic
That conflicting place
Of sinister taste

As the intensity rises
I wait for surprises
It came upon me
With spine chilling intensity
Beyond fear

Lurking in the shadows
Never showing itself
Haunting

As the seconds tick away
A taste of happiness
Is all it takes
To take you to
That special place

———

SECRET SELVES

Characters move in and out of space
They define themselves with grace
Each one a mask searching
For something special
Something new
Someone who knows
That love can only be true

A pristine feeling overwhelms
The knowledge of secrets
Not yet there
The look in her eyes
When she lets down her hair
From here we can go anywhere

Perform for the moment as it arrives
In the new dawn it goes on and on
Child of power we have art to create
Our union will form a creation of its own

———

SERPENT

Be strong, be sure, be in command
Of every decision you procure
The multitude of levels
Are as intricate as they are complex

Call on the wild untamed night
So the beast can roam free
And do what it would please

The time is now upon us
Dramatic fitful scenes fuel
The explosive pull of the hedonistic fire

The cavalry arrives to save the wrecked soul
That needs alcohol to forget
While wading through abstract fields
My inner fires sang His songs

———

BLACK HEART

A typical situation in life
You actually think it's a lie
You really, can't really tell why

When you do something blind
Without even a clue
What is your heart
Saying to you

———

REALMS

Enter the realms of darkness
Follow me, come see
Sense a trail beyond despair
The morning light, the morning air

What could you hope to you find
In such an empty space
Imagine a future
As it takes place

Never to be in one space of time
Limitless voyage begins inside
Enter through the gate
Echoes the voice of fear
Enter at will
Begin to create

———

JUDGEMENT

The wroth of fire
Ancient fury
Order in the court
Of this bays jury

Finally I can appreciate the written word
I can feel it, it's not just heard
So in this moment
This precious moment
I just want to say
Make it real
Don't be afraid to feel

Did you ever really think
That you could go without
You see everything I say is true
Then you'll believe me when I say
I love you

———

OBVIOUS DECIET

Hear the secret voices whisper
Decipher the subtle coincidence
Does it mean something to you
What do I have to do
To help you break through

Come join me now
In this strange old place
Replace despair with a happy face

Night after night of toxic rush
When will it be enough
When you want too much you loose touch
Of what you need, want turns to greed

What do you search for when your nearly there
Is it a throne or dire despair
Feeling something special, feeling something sweet
Feel awareness leave you
The feeling turns concrete

Vague understanding of how it all works
We all have ambitions, I know how it hurts
Do you want to take it high
Take it all
Just try not to cry

———

RELIGIOUS FREEDOM

The empty house stands in peace
Memories of what once was
Feeble attempts to recreate the past
The reputation was just a farce

A sexual scent sparks you up
A moral question, a golden ark
Relinquish your memories to me
Only death can set you free

Demons ruled his heart
Cheated him out of the one thing that he longed for
Starring in the dark, dreaming of the sun
She would be the last one

My shit is missing, who do you trust
In this modern rush
Paranoid thoughts border on the edge
Miscomprehend

Take it straight, twist it into art
Like it or not love is an ark

———

RUSH

Here comes the sun
The cities shadows are looming
The days progress all too consuming
Who to see, what to do
Is it important, are you

To sit in a room
Or to walk through the streets
Of a city in seize
Sensing the doom

Time has frozen into an everlasting second
Only you can set yourself free
From the grip of your society
So many pressures so much stress
Only for the dollar will she undress

An Island in Greece, a city in seize
Two different places do they know peace
What's it all for the effort that they make
To make it right, with what is wrong

I have many names
I am he
I am she
I am whoever
You want me to be

Quick silver modern dress
Shall she stop or shall she undress
Shall I stop now or shall I continue
In this hell my kitchen spell

Stop now or I shall protest
This silken weave
This simple dress

In this modern city
Is she blessed
All these morals
All these laws
Is she a virgin
Or is she a whore
Open the doors
Did you hope for more

———

REFLECTION

There's reflection in the waters
There you'll see those tired eyes
Those old Generals and their daughters
They're too tired to see the sky
Now there'll be no big surprise
Those old Generals and their orders
Now there's tear drops in her eyes
What your eyes cannot see
Look at with your mind
And what your mind cannot see
Feel with your hands heart and soul

———

ID

Truly dark children of the night
Respond to its calling
To the dawning of night
Despair is everywhere
You may hide but never escape
Its earthly embrace
Learn to love all that you would hate
Remember you can never escape
Worthless digit with no occupational title
Has no name
In this incessant game of capital gain
Stick to your guns
Remember its fun

———

MR REPORTER

How does one day turn into the next
How much pain do I need to express in this gentle
sentence
How can I endure her not being here year after year
The cold seems to penetrate my soul
It makes me shiver
It makes me twist
It makes wonder
If I'll ever feel her gentle kiss

———

PURE

Man goes on in his stillest moment
He endures his loneliest hour
To share love again
Emotions will come
Then they will go
The body that held them
Will learn to let them flow
The longing for love
Can get confused
The need for a body
Can lead you to blues
Look for a love
That will never let go
A special emotion
That knows how to flow

———

ARROW

Arch your mind into a bow
The rainbows reflection
Performs its show
Take these simple words
And make them fly
Look into heaven
With your inner eye
Virgin woods house
An angelic spring fed lake
In an untouched natural paradise
Snatch an opportunity to forgive a mistake
This pristine goddess that man seeks
Can she exist in this mortal abyss
It grows bigger everyday
It hungers it twists
With your mortal hand release your grip
Let the arrow fly
If you find her
You'll be fully equipped

———

ARK

Your eyes are saying something
That your smile is confirming
Your beauty is spiritual
I know I have found
A golden vehicle
For my love
I look for the smile
That you give me
When we're alone
It's how I'll remember you
When you're gone
Delicate warmth of divine power
Radiated love onto us
We nurtured it patiently
Lovingly forever after
Surrender to her exotic beauty
Her love is exquisite
It has no known limit

———

VALIENT MEN

A woman at night
A woman alone in the night
Stalking a most delicate plight
Aware that a spirit of fear
Could invade her here
Take caution my dear
For alone out here
Men can provoke the most dangerous fear
Alone in the streets at night
She walks down a dangerous line
Always on the edge
Please men don't pretend
Look within your hearts
Protect the scared Ark
Valiant Men
Take up arms against your enemy
A spiritual sword
A prayer to God
A shield of faith
And the power of Love
Let no man fail
That is pure of heart
Fight for HaShem
His golden Ark of Love
Let no guilt pervade you
If you are pure of heart now
Then let it be so
Let your heart be as Gods
Walk with Him
For the rest of your lives

———

DARK STAR

You have a God given talent
Do you feel like your wasting it
I feel the power of eternity on me
Be inspired by your story
It's yours, live it, sing it, understand it
Learn to live it with God
He is Love He is the way
Eternity is a long time
HaShem all the way
Get it right, keep it so
Then you'll see how to reap
Watch us grow
I love you now I'll love you then
I won't pretend this is not the end
Thank you for your peace
I'll sleep with grace
Amaze
She likes the light
So shine it bright
No words no lies
Give away your sins
Be free stay clean and dream
When the stars fall from Gods eye
We'll begin you and I
Don't think feel it
Cast out Satan
With the Love of HaShem
Live in blessed peace
Feel the powerful union of God
This is for the rest of your life
Now that you're a star

THE BROKEN

What you call liberal could be desensitization
Do you get offended by the violent and the negative
Or are you used to it
Trapped by it
Sensitive beings feel things in a different way
Stronger 'n deeper
It makes for week knees
How do we achieve all we have to achieve
To appease all these broken

———

OUT CAST

My flesh has demons I can control
It's through the flesh
We yearn, earn 'n learn
Heavy lessons are learnt
And then we're born
Something good is never scorned
Rejoice in what you have learned

———

SOMEWHERE

Dream of a place that no-one has been
Along with no others not even in dreams
Now that I have your attention
Let me ask you
Have you been
Is something real if it is not seen
Or what if you heard it
Was it a dream
What if it touched you
On the palm of your hand
Run away screaming
No way to understand
A gentle caress
On a magnificent dawn
Warm golden sunshine
Beaming on a suburban home

———

FRIENDS

We lost the eternal moment my friends
My ancient gold feathered
Float rafting friends
You where all so divine
My reason for rhyme
Now I have cried
For the loss of love
Ones I'll never forget
To go back and get
In touch with

———

PIT

I reach for the sky
From a bottomless pit
My passion is limitless
I succumb to times subtle embrace
I fall from grace
I fell into a hole a long time ago
So I created a show
Now I'm half way up the bottomless hole
Let my darkened heart speak
From within it's open door's weep
For loves gentle fate
Await, awake 'n seethe
Those who do not believe
We need a trigger to spark
A spiritual revolution
Is Gods word a solution
Why not hear Gods word in your heart
Make a vowel to the scared Ark
Carve a path into the dark

———

MR REPORTER

How do they climb onto the page
These words
Flying through my mind
On waves of emotion
A sequenced scene
Of the perfect world
Golden resplendent a dream
A pinnacle costs
Replace what is lost
What better place to start
Other than the empty recesses of your heart
Fill your world with love 'n zeal
What is left
Lead and steel
What about you Mr. Reporter
What do you feel?

———

TV WAR

Mans best friend TV
I can feel the gentle breeze
A draft rushes in
I sneeze
A tisshoo, a tisshoo, we all fall down
I can hear the words of war
A horde rushes in, it begins
Who wants to win
A victory begins with death
Who is blessed?
Those whom bring freedom at the price of death
Or those whom offer death as freedom
Look at all the rich people
Suckling at the beautiful world
Some more than others
Some more frenetic
In their lives
Because we like to cry
We keep the blinds drawn
A devil is spawned
Look at the infinitesimal nothing
It becomes obscure
A lure

———

OBLIVIAN

Your beauty is wondrous, glorious, splendour
As soon as I think it
It fades from my mind
Your wonder
Your splendour
Cannot be captured
In any rhyme

―――

PURGE

It's that feeling of complete exhilaration
And joy that you cannot contain
I feel the pain
There is energy contained
That cannot be stored
The more it is sought
The more resplendid it's heat
No need to speak
Now that you're into the jive
Let's dive
Let's submerge
Purge
All that is known
Enter the unknown
For it is only when you are free
From all you understand
That you can comprehend
All that is true

———

DESTINATION

Ancient wisdom
Distant voices
Dark wild bred
Untamed horses
Through the valley
Through the hills
Through eternity
Red blood spills

Glory to God
For He is almighty
He can do incredible things
Through simple people
He is simply almighty God

Let the angels sing
Let the heavens cry
And in one movement
Let our collective soul fly
Towards our Lord
HaShem

———

TOAST

So much to hope and strive for
Works of art we love to posses
A stranger starts to undress
Ambiguities are subtly interwoven into sheets of love
Smugly croon whilst darkness swarms in

Is strength to endure pain
Do you run from pain
Do you run from love
Subtle deceit, lovers can cheat
Fun'n games fan summers heat

Blood runs free
Love is its own decree
Don't tamper with me
Let truth shine
For truth and honesty are the only things
That can bear the weight of pure love

Can you love that which cannot be understood
Ghosts haunt men
Men write with pens
They endear themselves to their host
We all drink 'n clap to the appropriate toast

———

FLY

The days of merriment
The hours postponed
The projects we made
Into the night are thrown
We claw through each second
Feeling the way
The harder it gets
The more we pray
An inner passion
Feel it stir
The need to scream
A lonely bird
To live in the safety of
A precious net
Do you look at the world
For what you can get
Disguise the mood
Music soothes
An outward mask
Internal farce
Sugar coated dreams of love
Come crashing down
If I find her
I'll spread fairy dust
All over her wings
So she can fly
Memories haunt me from the past
Let's see some teeth
Let's end the farce
Translucent night open us up
Prepare us for flight
Prepare us this final time

MAN

What of man
What of the brotherhood of man
I ask you, I beseech you
Is there no solution to the chaos that consumes us
Cannot you man stand together with another man
In harmony
It's time for us mere mortals
To divine what should be
Through a sentiment of equality
It really must be
Acceptance is yours
Grow out of what you most despise
Moving through the times at such a rapid speed
So much going on instils reasons to exceed
In conversation love grows
A sudden pause
A shade of death shows
A pale comparison of what your heart expects
Think about what to feel next
Gently feeling subtle moods
The teeth are showing
Play the blues
Live each day for what its worth
Divine nectar is always there
Don't you run
Don't you dare

———

WOMAN

I dwell in darkness
It's where I lie best
Can't face the truth
Its brilliance is blinding
I was alone and yearning on a picturesque winters
afternoon
A feeling overcomes me in my solitude
A vision of another time
It's like remembering a past that you never thought you
had
Psychedelic scenes beyond comprehension
No meaning is meant that's why it exudes that special
scent
Get a grip you're up to your neck in it
What is there to say that hasn't been said
How many ways do we know how to pray
Wouldn't we rather take it instead
What is it you want that you pray for
That you work a hard day for
If it was only knowing that we knew
What would we do
Life is exciting, life is alive
The rotting love exhumed a perfumed stench
In a desperate and silent race
We move to appease our hearts
Silent fictitious dreams stirring in a hot sullen breeze
Why should I be so accosted
For two nights and two days did his soul solider on
But the moment grew more insistent
Demanding recompense
The agony came calling
Seeing her eyes everywhere

Thinking of only her
Wondering how I could make such a tragic mistake
The love I felt must of meant something
How could it come to this
Such loss

Such liars our most proudest selves
If only I could agree with myself
Pain aligns the ignorant
Suddenly a beautiful feeling of happiness envelopes you
Succumb to it, bath in its golden essence
Love is there to teach you how to love
Not to taunt you
To walk alone until I find the way back home
I'm happy as long as I don't realize it
For when I do I despair at the thought
Happiness leaves me and I await its return
I love you, can't you see, it radiates from me
You see these words but do you connect
Abstract fields of amber grey
Lucidly dream the day away
I play a central role, I manipulate, I control
Secret thoughts of high command
Make it so, wave your hand
Stretching and yawning
I great the day
At six in the morning
Eternity is another day
I confessed that I did love her
I asked her if she could see
But she did not answer me
She said "excuse me"
Is time the judge of love
Does she sit in judgment of me
And then hand down a sentence

To not have her is to ache
To be in her arms is splendour
Her embrace is as intoxicating as Gods would be
Her porcelain beauty, her classic shape
Does she not see the terror rippling through me
My vulnerable soul, delicate as the wind
The sorrows of my mind
Play these songs of madness

What until now has been truth
That which we seek
Us seekers of truth
Changes
What do you want to believe
Is what you choose to believe truth
Be wise in your judgment
For wisdom is sound
The sound of the wind
Echo's in the depths of my soul
Open your heart
Choose the right path
HaShem is Love
Time is the enemy of reason
Think not of why or how
Think of how long
Time is much like hunger
It cries to be satisfied
Which of course it never is
I will hold her love as sacred
Don't request it, don't ever test it
Take it for granted, her love is sacred
The unpaid servants did their work dryly
A course connected through a pattern
How did it happen
No one knew how we got through

I am not the way I am by choice
But by nature
Forgive me my aggression
It comes from too much passion
Not from malice, it hurts me more
I love her that I know
Why I do is highly disputable
There are too many reasons
Too many insignificant details
That set my heart on fire
My longing for her is strong
Stronger than my own strength
Perhaps that will be my final undoing
I do not wonder anymore
I only commit
For a tree to grow a seed must be planted
In order for love to grow reason must have departed
No logical mind can resist falling time after time
At the eye of the storm all is calm
It's where the wind blows that the damage is done
Be gentle with my love for it grows from the heart of a
dove
Innocent and pure my sins are fewer
With your love I'll resurrect my broken soul
That never really knew love before
The time is at hand to make my final stand
Will she adhere to such a love
Or is she casually passing
Trying to kill the dove
There is much folly in so sensitive a nature
It is not by choice that I dwell in deep chambers of
sorrow
It is by design that I seek so true a love
Every second without her is an
hour in sorrows chamber
My sweetest most delicate rose

Your love is an ocean to me
I could never drink it dry
Although I will eternally try
The tree of love is a rose bush
Has it been stated before
I assure you I'll love you more
This most noble prize guarded by thorns
Dealing with the pain is part of the game
All your misgivings haunt me, all your words of doubt
Crash upon my soul like bricks that you throw to guard
yourself
Be not weary of your pain for it is your love
I'll bleed for you eternally
Hour after hour until you finally succumb
And then deaths cool hands
extinguish the hot blistering
pain
That's how it must be
Who ever said love was free
Everything must be paid for in this life
For my love death is the price
I must have patience for my love to grow
The angry demons the destroyers of love must go
A garden of thorns is never exposed
Until you are pricked
Then the blood drips red and pure
To heal the wound with time
A train leaves the station, aboard is the love of a man
Each second it grows more distant
Each yard the sorrow grows more intense
I must put love far away from my mind
And keep it in my heart
For if thought of too long demons will start to paint
crimes
Scenes of horror from the imaginative depths
My heart grows weary from waiting

With understanding we grow day by day
Move away from the horrors of the mind that constantly
Want to climb into the light of our minds
I'm embracing the love around me
Keeping my mind free and pure
The mad rapture of grief keeps me sustained barely
For all things that are to be
They must already be
For they must grow eternally
Silent patient longing lies dormant
Until the rose beckons you
If tears must be shed
Then the soul will have bled
My soul cries for you
I sook and I spook
My soul cries for you in my sleep
A vision of you through tears
Surrounded by friends I broke and I wept
Kneeling before you I gave all I had left
To lose you is to surely die
I can't explain why
But for you girl I would gladly die
My darkest hour will be when I lose hope
Of ever being with you
On this hour I will lay down my human life
To another place I will progress
May humanities remaining hours be blessed
Oh divine structure that determines it so
I pray to you for peace and above all else
That the serpent does not catch the mouse
The world is a playground

———

DEATH

The poem I never sent you
Tears that blessed you
Time is eternal
Forever in each others arms
Crafted words
Sculptured songs
I secretly love it
I understand it
I never believed
I just see it
Best left unresolved
Never told
A dark secret
Never to be exposed
Sit in the shade, it's a different vibe
Try and stay alive
Anything could strike me now
Forget all this
Ask me how
I've reached an impasse
A strange arrangement with myself
A night could be forever
If I'm not in your arms
What foul presence has arrested me now
Disgraceful behaviour, confused words
What could be worse
Now it's time, now it's real
Come on baby what's the deal
Don't leave me hanging
In this tortured place
Give me a sign, pick up the pace

Master of mistakes
Everything you do makes you blue
How much pain do you need
Feel your heart
Constantly bleed
Think of me baby
I know it hurts
But it gets worse
Don't dispose of those you know
A mighty rage
A humble sage
Good night sweet heart
It's time to die
Good night sweet heart
A chance to cry

———

STRIKE OUT

Caught in time, transpose each day
Greeting the gift, each hour each shift
Now that my love is here my presence of mind is clear
Every time I taste her we touch
The sweet scent of her breath fills me with joy

Senseless movement into the pit
Losses of control, emotional flip
My heart is filled with darkness
At this apparent act

What you see as indecisiveness
Could be portrayed as posturing
What is in your heart
Beneath the spiky shell
Secrets you dare not tell
Beneath the oceans
Beneath the seas
Under the well
The moment you begin to tell
It couldn't be you
It couldn't be true
The karma we carry can't be ignored
The closet has many doors

REAL LOVE

Let Gods love heal
Take us past the point of no return
Let's not talk, let's not speak
Let's not go over the same old things
That makes us feel defeat
The bitter sweet of the sinless sleep
Can hurt your mind but not your soul
I love you baby
Have control

———

DREAMS

Here's some quiet reflection about life that you can
reflect on
Sssshhhh!! Thunderous rapture
Conceal your silent applause

Power to feel anger
Power to feel rage
Power to be humble
Do you know you're alive?

Come ecstasy
Give me this
Soft warm sullen kiss
I've got a taste for a vibe
It makes me feel alive
Yes an endless cultural cascade

Melt into a scene
Pick up the vibe
Scope the dreams
A frenetic frenzy
Of pumping bodies
Sweating, drinking
She's right in front of you
You want to connect
The hustling crowd
Moves you away
She's a walking dream
A modern woman
On the scene

———

MY BUTTERFLY

Butterflies fly naked through my eyes
Each one a different colour
But there is only one
Of a certain hue
It can only be you
My love is in my heart
And you have it for keeps
He could reason
He could rhyme
It started at the end
I won't try to pretend
Time becomes relevant
And you all know
It was his new piece
A slice of life
A piece
The sensuous feeling of being alive
Only comes when you are free
The sight of attraction gives you a rise
You're in the game
You're alive
Are you free?

I feel like I've just gotten to know you
Finally seen you smile
I'm opening my heart
Surrendering my disguise
Precious summer hours
It's funny how life goes sour
Obstacles to overcome

———

TALK WITH GOD

To all who fear deception, fear will blind you to the
truth
I can see both dark and light
I can see through you, see your darkness I can, can you?
I love you
Oh little child, why do you pretend
This is not the end
Not till I say, I will have my way
So stay, go on be bold, do what you are told
Do not stray, for I am not far away
Sit centred, do not be rocked
For I have the strength to see you through, for what I
have to do
Remember and marvel at the miracles I have unravelled
to you I will stay true
Let's talk about the most amazing things
Nano technology, particle physics
These are not to be marvelled at
But the fact that they where created is the marvel and
the marvel is God

Wake up and see, you can stop the misery
An open heart to me can set you free
In the name of HaShem you can be saved
The time has come so do not be late
I know who I am
A being with a name
A special name with special meaning
A being in carnal flesh that is teaming with God who
knows what to do
I sit patiently and wait for you
I love you Lord
I would wait fifteen years to spend one with you
I walk the streets by day with the Lord guiding my way
Gee it's cloudy today, I hope it doesn't rain
But know that if it does God will wash away my pain
I walk with the spirit without any fear
The happiness it brings gives way to a tear

———

GIRL

She knows true love to be
A mortal man on earth and free
She loved the Lord with all her heart
He sought her love His golden Ark

How could this be
What has occurred that you should be
So free

You are instilled with divine wisdom
And you use it with such love
Your passion sets my soul alight
Young free and empowered
Able to inspire a nation
You know what to say
And how to say it

Girl your faith is so strong
The purest I've ever seen
Your words strike at my very heart
Girl you are set apart

For you girl I would die
For you know HaShem
And He knows you and I

Together we could make the most awesome team
But I know that it might just be a dream
So I'll support you till the very end
And hope that in heaven we can be friends

All the raindrops in the entire world
Could not measure up to the tears I have shed
For joy and not for sorrow
Because I know you have love straight from above

Your love will lead many to the Lord
Your love is too precious for just any man
Your love is for God to command

———

Inspired by Linda

STAR

Come on star
Where going to heaven
Don't swallow the pill
It doesn't have to be uphill
It doesn't cost to get there
And it's already free
So you can't scare me
I'm free
I will always be

Come join me, you're terms
All roads lead to you
You're beautiful
Stay true

Everybody's welcome
And His arms are open
I have belief in you
You're there
Your empty stare

———

GIFT

From Heaven
Gifts at our fingertips
In one voice
The heavens cry out Holy
We write a piece
Heavens bliss
And it goes like this
Holy Holy Holy
Is Lord HaShem

―――――

REVIEW

Send your review to www.magcorp.com.au

Printed in the United States
by Baker & Taylor Publisher Services